Lantern Lit series
Volume 3

Dog On A Chain Press

William Graham

Mat Gould

Alan Catlin

Copyright© 2016 Dog On A Chain Press

All rights reserved. This book or any portion thereof
may not be reproduced or used in any manner whatsoever
without the express written permission of the publisher/author(s)
except for the use of brief quotations in a book review.

Printed in the United States of America

First printing 2016

ISBN 978-0-9855291-6-1

Dog On A Chain Press
c/o Beasley Barrenton
503 Silverleaf Rd.
Zionville, NC 28698

For ordering information (Publisher Direct) or all other inquiry
dogonachainpress@yahoo.com
http://dogonachainpress.tumblr.com

for contributor credits/permission see back page(s)

"Put it to use be it cock or sword, flail not in earnest, leave no martyr unscorned, be born unto wolves"   Bazzel Bumgarden

"Now I see the night, silently overwhelming day"   Bob Kaufman

Renegade Ballads

Poems

by

William Graham

Salvage yard

From whatever can be found
salvage the wreckage and build.

Assemble a home
with broken boards
rusted tin
bent nails
old car seats and an eager hammer.

Swing furiously.

The thought constantly humming behind my ears

It would be easy
to continue walking tired and heavy
life long
every damn day
boots slowly collecting the muck.

The weight of that motion
growing with each lurching step
reminds me that I need to return
to grinding away for that which is loved ecstatic.

I'd rather be a beggar with an open hand
than a king who clings to his gold and crown.

It's a stupid way to carry on

Readily and openly I have waited
for the next great war seemingly looming.

I imagine tremors,
the plates colliding
and recessing to reveal the fires lashing out.

In my mind and heart
I often live like I have already died

and if I were to give some final words
they would be this:

This is not a way to live, my friends,
this isn't a way to die either.

AVOID:

Building the self a prison:
Leave when you can.

Kicking rocks with your head down:
This ain't a way to wear in your shoes.

Eating rotten fruit:
Throw out that shit and grow something new.

Hell and Brimstone:
Keep setting fires though.

Bandages:
Give the wounds some air.

TO GET BY:

Be friends with yourself.

Kill the idea that you are your own worst enemy,
give yourself a deep bottom-of-the-lungs inhale
for freedoms sake.

Sometimes you are your own cruel captor,
be a gracious jailer and let yourself come
and go freely.

I'm often reminded

You grow attached
and you can't help it
to not would be against our nature.

I tell people that it becomes
near impossible to judge anyone
the longer you listen to their stories
the more you hear
the more the lines between
his or hers and mine and yours
are commonplace

until there is no longer any difference between them.

they made choices
you made choices
good ones
bad ones

circumstances and details may have been different
but the choice was essentially the same.

Keep it

I would leave my home and drive,
on days when stirring from desperate sleep
was a drawn out chore

early as it was,
the sky was nearly always the same
great hands splashed bleeding water colors
across its deep and sad blues.

as cold as it was,
I would reach my thieving hands out from the window
plundering all that I could for myself
every fist full packed tightly into my pocket

firmly pressed against my leg
fabric staining, as the stolen contents
slowly dissolved into my skin.

Veterans Day talk radio

On the air, a matter-of-fact,
war torn, time rebuilt voice
spoke with certainty
of the battles won and blood lost.

Here was simplicity:
Short sentences with heavy burdens
bound to each word.

I survived.
they did not.
I have felt
that
loss.

Here, something sacred

Well tended fires hiding
within a darkened forest,
faithful ghosts warm and close

crouched low, clawing through
the thickets keeping me from them

in my pocket
a box of strike anywhere matches
I take one out, the rest a row of soldiers at attention

one as kindling
for the next and the next and the next
for as long as the box will last.

Bears

Goddamn,
day in and day out,
this incessant horde of bears

in my yard
tearing through the trash
that I always forget to take to the dump.

Tattered

The light only touches a few things
on the other side of this window pane.

First being the mournful dust against the glass
dry rivers
written histories

a season hot and arid
a season of rain
again a season of heat.

Second, the cobwebs,
a loosely spindled trap in the corner.

And third, the moth, from which I cannot look away
desperate wings tangled.

I wish it would remember to rest.

Grey

Before the winter arrives
I forget what movement looks like
the land, given fog,
is no more than blurred
and then all together grey
in the type of way
in which you can stare
in one direction
for hours
and never see a damn thing
but at the same time see everything.

How a possum dies

Coming home after work to a locked house
windows shut the whole place dark

no one expects to turn on the kitchen lights
and find two black and ugly eyes
staring at you
from the counter top

greedy paws
clinging to the loaf of bread
left on the counter.

It was good to see you

I walked in afraid
with millions of miles of thoughts and questions
and saw the weathered and alive soul
of your solemn face.

words
only a drop in the barrel of myself
a simple acknowledgment,

strong enough
to instigate stagnant waters,
trouble the doldrums

and excite the winds again.

Death, another beautiful necessity

Walking toward as well as away,
clenched fists holding hands
one softens the other.

Breathing is comprised of duplicate measures
taking in and letting go.

These tiny sacraments seem insignificant,
but it is in this sense we live.

Exodus 16:4

24 hour grocery stores.
And sushi.

24 hour grocery stores
that carry sushi.

Delicious crunchy wrap sushi.

Accessible
24 hours

every
single
day.

Oh my Lord you are gracious indeed.

This coffee tastes like unrequited love

You make my espresso shots
and hand me a paper cup
to fill with dark coffee

sometimes I add cream
rarely any sugar.

I read you sonnets and kiss your face

that's about it though.

…unrequited love (part 12)

I've never met you
I know this
but I wanted to tell you

the other night I had this dream
as silly as it sounds
we sat in the kitchen
speaking little
but smiling softly.

We shared an orange
between the two of us

how sweet it was.

The means

Whether your hands are honest or not,
come along side
to put down your endless work

and take these stale old words,
rotting on our tongues for so long
and help find the means

to distill all
down to what they were meant to be.

William Graham is currently dwelling in the rural sticks outside of Boone, NC. He works at a homeless shelter and in his free time apprentices under a sculptor/blacksmith. He is still trying to figure out what this whole poetry thing and spends his days pondering the whereabouts of such questions with a somber heart.

William recently published "Setting The Hillside Ablaze" a Zine compiling his personal Appalachian born poems of soul searching and treasure hunting, too which –TO GET BY- first appeared and was the catalyst for this publication with *Dog On A Chain Press*.

BONE CHIMES HECKLING THE REMNANTS OF A DYING BRIGADE

poems by

Mat Gould

the shade tree is under me

the sun is bestial

the son of celestial deeds
laughingly provoked by sin
that which is feign to begin with

needing to rely
why call it anything but love

celebrate the heat
speaking inherently repeat after me

only the sweat from off of our brow may save us now

the parched fields lie silent
relying on need
there is no rain dance for the devout embattled-

resurgence

bodies of water need rivers
that need tributaries

my body needs a reservoir of light

no sinking peril
reaching deep, irretrievable
narrows
at arms-length, separation

unplug the well dam,
the damn well is not dry
only low

a gurgle fills the bucket, spills
out the spout
onto the ground-

putting out the embers

wet cloth beating
smoke language speaking into the empyrean dusk
folding under the mountains ridges

the clouds are dry
it is hard to see them without most of the moon projecting through

asunder from periphery
paw prints elude following
strictly from where I can see
and away from the smoldering fire

guided
by
eyes ignited
a bellow, a brawl, the clamor of a mating call-

soup chicken

gizzard pulled
water boiling against mediocre air
steam sizzling, a horn pules

with pugil stick I swing at beast, a figment wails

heart and liver, scourings for the descendants of myth
under the cliff crying aloud
kill stiff

hanging from sturdy limb as mention of warning

critter must be swift, brave
or silly with dementia
if for a lick of salt to be pinched-

resonant

need
to change
the light
bulb
has gone
out

need to find one that lasts longer

lamp oil
is
better
wicks stay wet
hold in the wind

behind
thin
glass

burnishes through onto near-by
ordinary on the eye enough to read
or
even to carry out into the world
chasing apparition
looking for the lost

the unknown amongst them both

they were so close
until
night came between them-

don't get naked or ask for the truth

spinning
the bottle

nerving the shadows

so
as
to
pick
the next fight-

an entire subsistence

above the alter, the heads of the hunted
their glassed eyes holy with reflection,
horns sharpened, ready for weapon.

what of the rib?
all of any of the other bones?
the earth is a rapid digester.

yet a few adorn totem
a few hang from chest
a few held by the hand holding the ritual staff
under coyote head dress a wraith with a rattlesnakes face.

but what of the other bones?

a few stir bowls
a few pin the hide
a few made into arrow, drawn back, deep toward the shoulder,
held tight, slung shot.

more bones for prayer
more bones to accompany the chant-

dinner scraps

something carrying itself heavy ran through the cockleburs
I turned the porch light on a minute or so after I heard it
the genius of a nonchalant and slightly drunken motive

there is an excess of debris upon the ground right now

whatever animal went crashing through abounding
I did not hear it cross the road
it may have gone into the culvert
or it could have softer steps than supposed

I stood on the stoop
figuring it to be monstrous
blew out the lantern

and let it live to be so-

soot and cinder

the thin sticks are burning
they'll burn into a bigger fire
one that keeps well into the caverns recede
one that boils blood and purifies steel
a fire that leaves the days compromise complete

the thin sticks are burning
they'll burn into a bigger fire
hands held over
faces given lambency

ash is thought
there within is what matters

the thin sticks are burning
burning into a bigger fire
one kept with stones surrounding
one that will raise the night whooping of premonition
one that will keep its coals inspired until the pale dawn enlightens-

considering the vault

if anything was to be of ease,
I would land on my feet and hack away at ice cream hillsides
march with ants
and come back with their queen

my wager is a pearl

launching bottle rocket arrows at the animal spirits
lighting up their ghost
so I know where to go
when this happens to me

my wager is a pearl

I will accept, also the dime
coins add up
heavier with each one dropped into the bag

I keep mine buried in jars

my wager is a pearl
under which cup the ransom,
a head will lay handsomely upon a bosoms apostle-

apocalypse starting over

watery eyes in a dull rampage of clouded sky
a dry breath I am not getting back

up against the wall without a blindfold
which hand will your lover hold

no throat can swallow the thorough gutter full
a whole city bereft in a drizzle

a dirty cup of coffee
dim iridescent overtones

standing ovations
for a lap dance in the afterlife

a particular devil flashes his monocle
blushing with mania, fluently boozed

no shadow for the scrawny dog
silence is a bomb

ode,
if I never tell you it is because I mean every word

the sun struggling to punctuate the day
staying above ground just long enough to nudge the dust

oil and wine
thick and refined

I am starving for cold beans-

the grudge

night improves the fires light
smoke never really clears
bones are always burning

a sky swallows the world inside out

the cruel bargain of an 18 degree sun
kerosene in the lungs
the febrile tongue of miscreant season

winter's deprivation swells the eyes
the year has been long
but without measure
the days pass with minimal resistance

I will not come off of the hill
I will curse and groan
I will breathe carnal fume
I will sit back down with no milk

and scowl-

for those with very little love to leave behind

what was once known to be heartache
was only the breaking in of the heart
4 chambers
.20 caliber

the target trembling under breast

rabbit foot prints in the sleet, silt, or snow
it is blood that is tracked
leading back to a hole underneath the hunters feet
a good place to keep oneself

the beating cannot be heard

the laughter and the cries are a simile
brief to the ear
elongating a breaths serendipity
sifting through the imminent infinite
for what extinction hath discarded

a world of stray mutts
a border land for scavengers-

saviors stew

a sufficient journey will meet explicit need
a scuffle upon a brutal tundra

hunger
will
ail

the thickening heart will cackle

the day has been gutted
the meat has been chewed
it was gristle at best

if nothing else, a blessing
on the trail, surrendered by the blind
whom had found it first-

a murder convenes

Carrion was it you
who flew over and left your winged shadow
on the bare afternoon hillsides

seeking the wounded
or something off its guard
a fattened prey with saccharin on its rump

crows carry their bodies over the wilderness
fat black darts in the thin air
calling out for survivors of a heinous winter
vigilant to what there is left of the dead

it is hard to sense birth
marrow ravaged, bone hollow
a skeletal warrior laid to rest on the earthen floor

spirits perform in colors I do not see
silent praise gives way to a jesters guffaw-

give them blankets for one more day

cold flowers sitting up on the hill
held together, leaning against one another
they are not supposed to survive ice storms
they face a shrouded sun, they attempt to look up

I check back in on them later in the day

more bent
wilt settled, snow embossed
somehow a strength in their stem

not wanting to be slain unto the ground, shivering mad with lust,
cursing their affairs

they don't mean it, they are cold flowers,
flowers that are not supposed to be cold

ever so willing to come to life-

walking the ghost back home

doves do not only coo, they hack
just as coyote howls, cries, gragles and laughs

when men die they do not take their bones

birds hang supple from vines that do the same
berries in their beak, ransacked from the shrubbery
a hackneyed guard from a more engorged wilderness

what a man leaves behind
is not unlike what lies on either side of threshold or boundary

but when a man dies he does not take his bones

inferno burns most
but for a smudge
that then becomes a symbol of revelation or retribution

just as bottle trees and bowling balls are yard ornaments used for
iridescent gazing
or a steer head with broken horns serves as a scarecrow on a post
although, is that a crow I see perched on the barren brow?

tethered or whipped
be it stripped or stripping
what has lost its way or is it holy without guidance?

one mouse means more mice unless it is solely on its own
a mutt will only do so much from where it sits on the scape

and when a man dies
he does not take
his bones-

asteroid gravel

is
bigger than a grain
has sharp dimples yet soft weathered edges
is not moon stone
or river rock

will stain your bare feet so too will berries on your teeth
holds in steam as it is very tough to cool

is
combustible
when first dampened

is
similar to charcoal if need be burned again
does not work well in concrete mix

is best for drive-ways or long country roads that get little use

can be polished and worn as would a gem
leaves a chalkish residue
comes in multiple colors
and can be turned into lead for pencils

is
a bit extravagant
but cheap as marbles
yet
hard to come by-

patting myself on the back

do the dishes
step outside
smell the air
hope not to cringe
and figure this must be it

sitting on the porch,
in a mist of swelling humidity
while the green that comes before green was becoming greener in
its yellowness
and listened to some bird tell the world how beautiful it is.

now, too go pee on the lawn
it'll die down
and then a yawn, a big exciting yawn, regardless of it all-

solitary refinement

oblong sun polishing a stare
I could be wrong, it may be looking off to the side
wedged into a ridge

following along, down onto the waterside
where it becomes an entire lake
painting rocks the color they already are-

wandering through willows

I have never wandered through willows
although often,
I have wandered through those willows

willfully a portion of the mind
with no other reason to think bafflingly
of doing anything other

than wandering through willows-

Mat Gould's work is intently and intensely postured with stark recurrence and language that is formidably bred to be "subtly apocalyptic" in the sense that it is "the gospel of which we will always be singing" and regardless of such, there is the declarative presence of life and what must be done to incite it. Landscapes, character, and vision are often revisited with an understanding that there is an illimitable world amassing duality, thriving and suffering, evoking brimstone, hilarity, survival, and folklore. Somehow, both provocatively and simply, curated in brisk verse.

Gould has authored 4 books of poetry exclusively with [Dog On A Chain Press](). . **Bone Chimes**…is a companion piece to his inclusion for Lantern Lit Vol. 1.

Mat Gould lives half way up a gravel road on the other side of a mountain in Western, North Carolina where he keeps a steady yet at times drunken aim eye on his own. He is currently whittling poem into a sharp point.

Empty Glass Epilogues

Poems by

Alan Catlin

Oh lucky men

Some say it the luck of the poets,
not necessarily the Irish, though some
of the poets were, without a doubt, Irish.
Lucky the way Berryman was lucky,
as he waved, witnesses said he actually did,
before jumping from a bridge over the
muddy Mississippi . Or lucky like Lowell
was in love and family wars, talented wives,
all three of them, novelists, though he stole
from personal letters from the second wife
to write of the soon-to-be-third, one of
the most awful books ever. Lucky dying
in a cab, returning to the second with a portrait
painted of the third, painted by her previous
husband, one of the most renowned artists
of his time. I often wonder whose property
that painting became and how much it was
sold for given how L. Freud's go for millions
apiece, then and now. Or lucky like Delmore,
feted young as both a poet and a prose stylist,
whose dreams ended irresponsibly, in a pauper's
rat hole. Or lucky like Jarrell, whose drinking
helped fuel his acerbic reviews but not the poems
he no longer wrote, dead before his time,
either by accident or design, beneath the wheels
of a car. Or lucky like Hugo, sober for awhile
in late in life love and marriage, then back to
the sauce, master narrator of his fate, dead
of heart attack, no doubt aided by resuming
drinking. Or lucky like the silver tongue Welshman
who could always cadge a drink and charm a woman
to a bed, felled in a barroom one shot beyond
the bar record and not yet forty, though the poems had long ago
ceased. O lucky men, all of them, poets dying before their time,
drunk and disorderly, all of them. Their words supersede them.

Irish Rovers

"Don't put on any airs
When you're down on Rue Morgue Avenue...."
Bob Dylan

If they had a name these guys
would be called, The Dead Before
Death Gang. All of them aging
badly, an average of two ex-wives,
three point one kids. All of them on
probation, or just off for no support
paid, driving without, driving under
the influence of, the whole nine yards.
All of them thought they could have
been contenders, would have made
the team if it weren't, could have had
that job but, would have married the
girl they really loved if only.
All of them living fill in the blanks
lives, lists of if onlys like posted
legal notices in newspapers, their
lives foreclosed long before the fat
lady sang, the time clock expired,
the summons was handed over.
All of them knew every process
serving trick in the book, had even
invented a few themselves when they
were on the hook for a job and nothing
else was available. Washing dishes was
for wetbacks and they weren't going there
no matter how bad it got, could never
be that desperate. The stuff they wouldn't
do, hated worse than their own lives, could
fill volumes. Buy them a shot and a beer
and they'll be glad to recite the whole list.

The White Giant's Thigh

All the bar girls loved
his poor boy at the party
good looks: shaggy hair,
a few inches too long,
curling iron teased,
his weeks-without-shaving
beard shaped to look like
a six o'clock shadow,
his half glasses for reading
verses scammed from back
pages of college texts or
the ones he memorized like
"Do Not Go Gentle Into
That Good Night" or
"The White Giant's Thigh".
All those words he fathomed
his own with rich recitations
in deep baritone voice,
whiskey edged and cigarette
rough, a pint a poem he never
pays for. All of the breathless
women dying to run hands
beneath bleached-to-a-stylish-
fade t-shirt that said:
"Poets Do It With Words".
After he's had them all,
he returns to his spot along
the rail with the battle tested
boys who buy him rounds
for last call, savoring all
the details he tells and whatever
he withholds: Into Her Head
Lying Down, dreaming of
the land where their ancestors
lived and they were young
and wild and the world was
full of promise for a greener day.

Hart Crane's Bridge to Nowhere

The voyage out of his mind
was a champagne glass filled
with bootleg gin, false laughter
at sad jokes no one knew the point of,
elaborate meals that seemed to stretch
from midnight to dawn, the captain's
table overturned for dancing couples
as a female singer closed her eyes
and sang as "The Band Played On."
His many notebooks, journal pages,
filled with scribbles, parts of poems,
obscene doodles, illegible sketches
that suggested a vast architecture
of nothing, a monument to defeated
dreams, struts and steel casings,
snapped cables of suspended visions.
Out there, somewhere, beyond the first
class cabin windows, the polished railings,
a churning wake, the tidal waves,
answers to questions posed except
the unspoken, the ultimate one
that supports the bridge between here
and nowhere.

L. Cohen's First European Tour

All along the watchtowers, the Martello
ones facing the sea, gun slits for eyes
viewing the garbage in the harbors,
world war ruins, the ones just past
and the ones to come, that first European
tour the backup band felt as if they were
playing one venue and the singer another,
summers of love ending in ashes,
Isle of Wight in the rain, a long, extended
suicide note, a bad trip even without lysergic,
stoned reflections in muddy water.
Not quite the prophet, then, or is it, yet?
ascending the tower of song. The last
gig, and probably the best, in an institution
in London, "I really wanted to say that
this is the audience that we've been looking for.
I've never felt so good playing before
people before." The asylum of song, crazy,
man, crazy.

Portrait of the Artist a Few Weeks Prior to His Death by Misadventure

"Words come with afternoon,
the grammar if forgotten, stream
of consciousness, of scotch."
　　　　Leslie Anne Mcilroy

His face bloated by years of drowning
all the words that refused to be rescued
in whatever-was-on-offer-as-long-as-it-
was-alcohol. Endless days and nights
of pub crawling, offering himself as
entertainment in lieu of writing anything
down. IOU's cheerfully offered
for funds for short cigars, cigarettes,
a pint or six, collector's items now,
as no one dreamed he would ever repay.
Especially not the poet, in last week's soiled
clothes, rank with perspiration and spillage,
brown eyes culled by a cataract of malt
whiskey and ale, his uncombed hair receding,
permanently ruffled by sea air or willing
partner's at pub crawl's end. His full
lips swollen, stained a sick off-yellow
mix of nicotine and HEP3, subject to
the general bloat of a body awash in
booze and about to fail in mid-swallow.

The Three Burials of Pablo Neruda

First order of business after the coup,
is all the opposition politicians are
to be collected and, no questions asked,
summarily shot. Then the journalists are
rounded up, the educators, the poets,
the musicians.

A man like Pablo, revered by the people, is more
than an inconvenience, more than a nuisance,
but a threat, to be eliminated less than two
weeks after previous regime's end and
buried as quickly, and as anonymously,
as circumstances allow.

Pablo dead, the official releases say, of prostate
cancer, which conveniently flared up and proved
fatal before Pablo could formulate a response
to circumstantial changes in government.

Still, 40 years later, on the eve of his third
burial, at his intended resting place on Isla Negra,
his chauffer tells of a so-called doctor's
visit, of a hypodermic needle applied to the poet's
stomach and the pain thereafter, horrible to behold,
the death throes, eternal dreaming in a minor key.

A quicker death, no doubt, than the suffering
endured by all the marked men, those poets,
musicians, philosopher's taken for final rides
in blue Falcon death squad cars to soccer stadium
for torture, humiliation, murder. Pablo spared this.
A kindness, no?

Pinochet would have said so, if asked, but who was
going to ask him?

The General's lips were sealed, covered by purple clothes,
to protect him from evil spirits that might seek
to inhabit his unwary soul, inhaled, as they often
are, in transition hours of any day, when day becomes
the blackest of nights.

Those spirits like words of the poet in his second
grave, among his ancestors, still composing verses
in his unease, trapped in a place where it is
neither day nor night, searching for a clear way out.

"dead friends, dead days, dead loves"

The scene was like stepping
inside a Russian novel, one like
<u>The House of the Dead</u>,
or <u>Cancer Ward</u> or perhaps
<u>Gulag Archipelago</u> primed.
Novels filled with characters
who were not quite dead yet
but who wished they were.
Characters who had woken up in
some place even worse than a
death house, spirits all around,
heavily armed with instruments
of torture, more Medieval,
more primitive, than anything
a Spanish Inquisition could have
devised. Lights inside this
place are incredibly bright,
flashing on and off at randomly
timed intervals, fit inducing
intense, and accompanied by
ear-bleeding loud, Post-Industrial
Death Metal Music, alternating
with monotone nonsense words,
spoken as if they were recitations
from some made-up-on-the-spot
satanic language uttered by fifty
shades of dead demons, their controllers
all in black leather suits trying to
induce everyone inside to reveal
secrets they might have once known
but no longer applied to anything
in this life. Not that what was said
was important, it is the process that
is important, not the actual message

and to think, you came here of
your own free will, sauntered up
to the bar, and ordered a specialty-
of-the-house, drink, and twenty years
later, here you are, wondering if there is any point in wanting to
leave to even dream of ever being anywhere else.

Guernica

" ...in my hometown
there's even a nightclub named
Guernica." Jessica Hagedorn

Where they play nothing but
dangerous music, atonal and
dissonant, so strident, unmuffled
ears bleed, are assaulted by solo
guitar riffs, percussive drum beats,
organ blasts; killer sounds one and
all. The bouncers are all armed guards,
uniform like Nazis. No one dares
to intrude, tries to leave once they
are locked in for a night of danger
and beauty, gangster love and heart
throbbing infarctions. The heat inside,
the unnatural light inspiring visions,
tropical apparitions vivid as death
squads, angels from hell with pilot's
licenses, machine guns and bombs.
In my town there is a night club named
Guernica where turf wars are fought
and lost, where the innocent plead
for mercy and are denied. In Guernica,
I am the demon on the dance floor,
the one with a coat of arms: blood
splatters on a field of clay.

A Room of One's Own

"If you believe in God, you'll believe in anything."
                    Joseph Torra

Lost weekend that became a fortnight,
waking up who-knows-where, washed
out and wary, time wiped away in self-
induced fugue state of alcohol and reefer,
pep pills and poppers. Clothes that smelled
of a season in hell spent crawling through
sewers with the rats, blood caked, broken
fingernails and slime coated skin, caked
lips and chipped teeth, trembling with
body heat, a need more pressing than
escaping from the cold. Amid torn pages
from dozens of books strewn about beyond-
filthy-squat, room, epic poems transcribed
from dictations from dead poets, reams of
writing, all of it written in words no one
was likely ever to decipher or to understand.
Not something from a pleasure dome decreed
but something by Rimbaud, as a gun runner,
dope sick and insane, or by one of those
Russian poets he had sent arms to, who
would rather blow their brains out than
write another word.

Mayakovsky at 3 AM

Eyes closed, stuffed head in
a noose, broken arms
wrenched aside useless as
foam, the smoke of many
cigarettes in glass ashtrays
on the littered, low table,
dealt playing cards folded
into hands, played tricks
amidst litter: empty clear
bottles, overturned shot glasses,
spent cartridges, dueling pistols,
barrels still crossed on the wall
above the torso of a bald,
black veiled woman, painted
eyes half-open, false lips
the color of dried blood.

Anna Akmatova 1998

The severed arm bent at the elbow
rests on the clock with one hand
pointing to 12 where time stopped
and became as unreal as the hollow
cavity in this detached arm, a place
just below the shoulder now stuffed
with a tidy spray of flowers where
bone should be, a bunch of green
grapes nearby and a miniature Venus
de Milo statuette facing away from
time; the displaced arm and hand
no longer able to caress the tortured face.

Dostoyevsky 2000

sits, head resting on gnarled
hands, dislocated fingers
bruised and discolored, a fan
of dead sticks, a nest hair
is growing on. Fledgling chicks
clamor for worms, the greasy
eels that slide from his ears
no bird would touch, remains
of a game of chance on the card
table he leans on, blank faced
black dominoes resting each
against the other, the low moan
of his mad teeth broadcasting
the daily news, affairs of state;
his mind clamors for it.

Pasternak Pastoral

The butcher's tools are all
spread about on the picnic
table: bone saws, hatchets,
seven sizes of filet knives,
each ready for the sectioning
of horses to be lifted from
their stables and hung about
their distended waists by cloth
straps, straw bouquets stuffed
in their mouths, heads draped
with dried flower garlands,
their eyes swollen by fear
bulging like fists wrapped tight
in white gloves, blood leaking
like glycerin tears, forged nails
hot from the blacksmith's fire
awaiting the hammer's blow.

Mandelstam's dream

of the red chamber where
the dead are stored, only
coming back to life to test
the love of those for whom
an embrace is a trial, an awful
test of will whose failure means
a choice of executions: a slow
one, unclothed, exposed to
the elements on a flatbed
Trans Siberian railway car
or up against a wall, fired bullets
melting like icicles in the heart.

Alan Catlin has been publishing for parts of five decades which makes him feel like the answer to a baseball trivia question. He can honestly say he is the only poet in the world who has published in the... *God's Bar Unplugged, Yammering Twits, Imploding Tie-Dye Toupee, Wormwood Review, the Literary Review and Wordsworth's Socks.*

His latest books are a full length one from *Lummox Press*: Last Man Standing and a shorter book: Beautiful Mutants from *Night Ballet Press*. Forthcoming in 2016 is American Odyssey from *Future Cycle Press*.

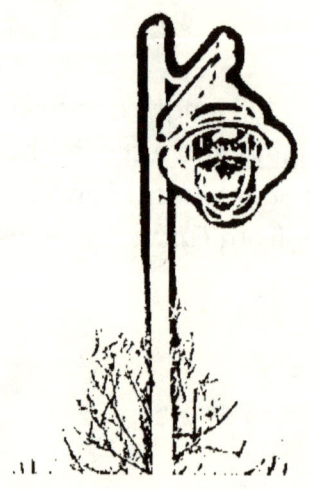

Above photo rendition: **Gabriel Santerno**

Cover Design/layout: **Ryan W. Bradley**

Dog On A Chain Press logo: **Valentine Cranford Reilly**

The manuscripts for this -Lantern Lit series- have been personally sought for their pelt, and selected by me with great interest and appreciation for poets that I am genuinely enthralled to work with, poets that are poets at the basis and gnarl of their being. Poets who cannot help but be such, poets that will continue singing the gospel, the gospel of which we will always be singing, poets commanding the ship from wherever it is that they may deliberate, roaring out to a bird on the wire as if that bird is everyman at the pier of their own existence.

Keep a lantern lit,
Beasley Barrenton

www.ingramcontent.com/pod-product-compliance
Lightning Source LLC
Chambersburg PA
CBHW031422040426
42444CB00005B/674